The Wisdom
of Babies

Life Lessons from the Diaper Set

LAINE CUNNINGHAM

The Wisdom of Babies
Life Lessons from the Diaper Set

Published by Sun Dogs Creations
Changing the World One Book at a Time
ISBN: 9781946732538

Softcover Edition

Cover Design by Angel Leya

Copyright © 2017 and 2019 Laine Cunningham

All rights reserved. No part of this book may be reproduced in any form or by any means, electronic, mechanical, digital, photocopying or recording, except for the inclusion in a review, without permission in writing from the publisher.

Introduction

Having a baby changes your life. It provides an entirely new perspective on why you are on this earth. No matter where your path led before your child arrived, cradling that warm bundle for the first time is transcendent.

All the things that don't really matter wash away. The center of your world shifts. Problems you worried about disappear, and challenges you never bothered to consider require your attention.

In the days that follow, it's easy to forget all the things you thought and felt during those first precious moments. The endless rounds of diaper changes, bottle warmings, and laundry threaten to wipe away that memory.

Amid the chaos, though, other treasures await: the way your child's eyes lock onto yours. That first smile. The gurgling coo of pleasure. Those moments can be as transcendent as your baby's arrival.

These experiences also offer wisdom...some of it funny, some of it profound. And because babies universally inspire wonder, their wisdom spreads beyond the parents. The lessons infants learn as they grow can keep us young at heart and help us grow in spirit. *The Wisdom of Babies* is as timeless as the cycle of life.

Drool is cool.

The heartbeat is
the primal drum.

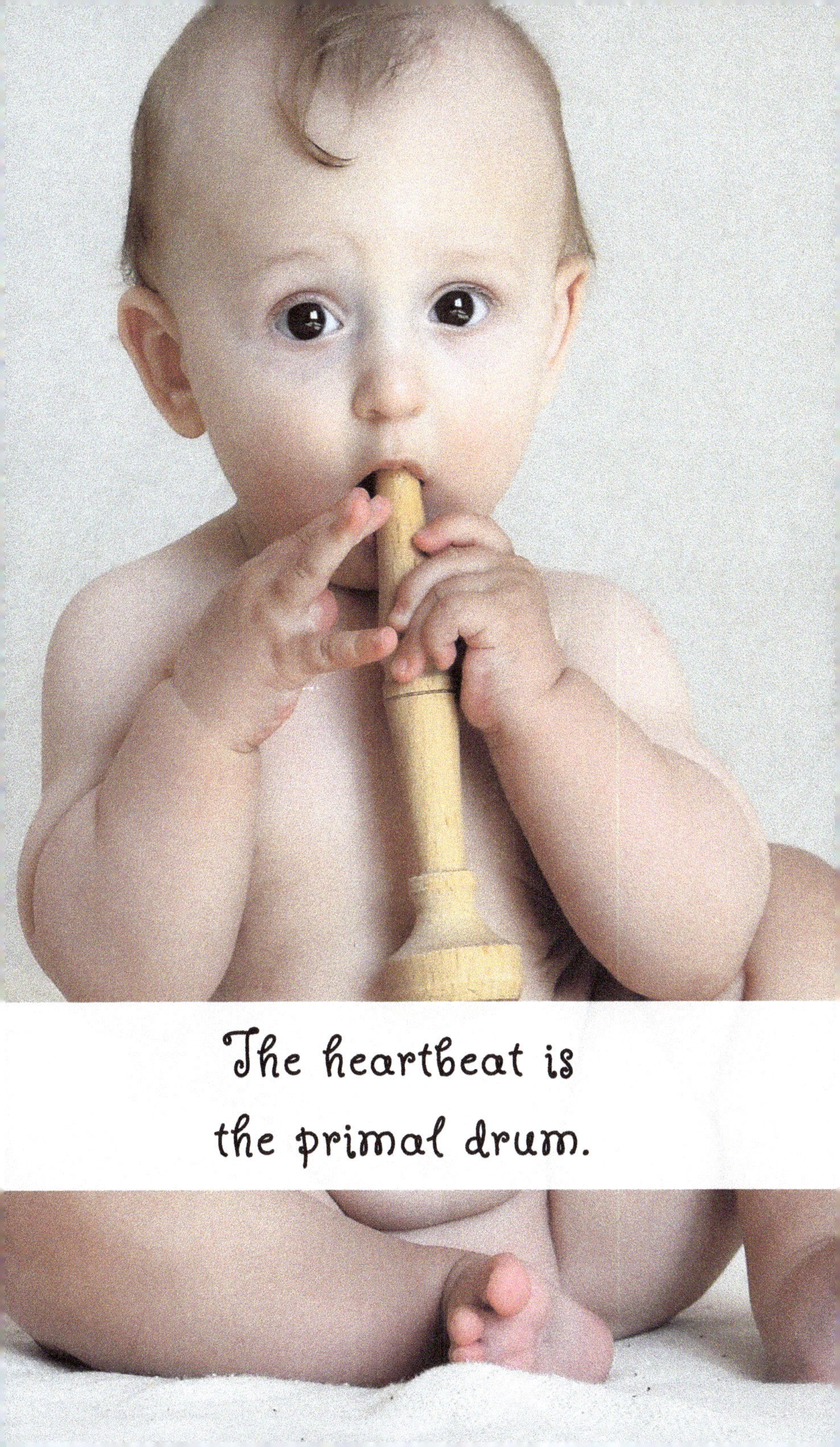

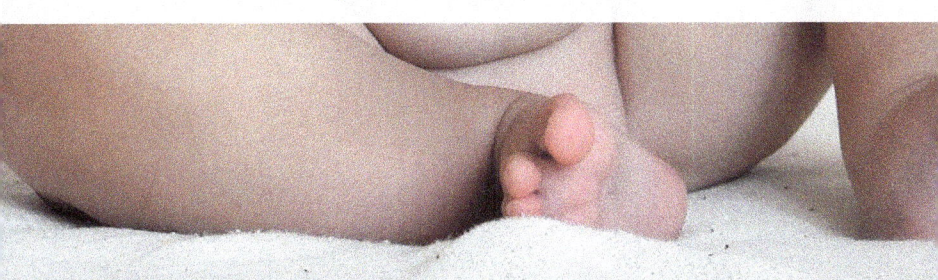

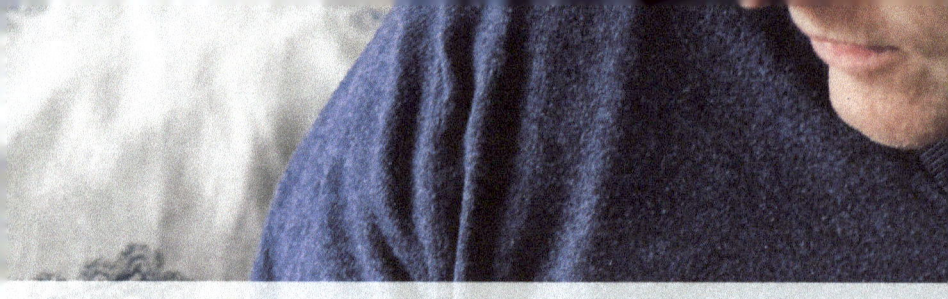

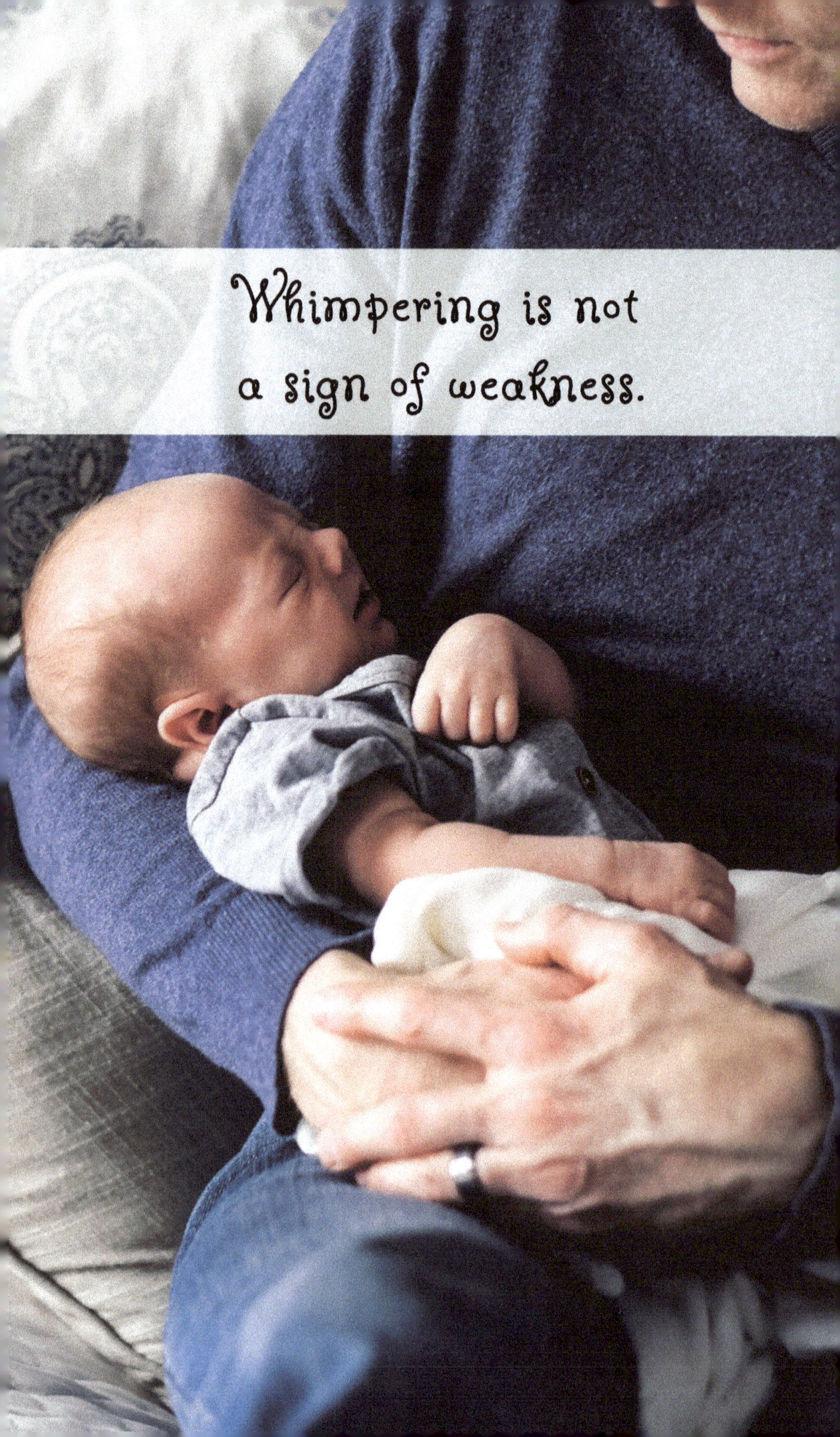

Whimpering is not
a sign of weakness.

Food is a full-body experience.

Being rocked is transcendent.

A dirty diaper ain't nothing but a thing.

Curiosity is required.

While learning to walk, you will occasionally fall down.

Babbling is a type of music.

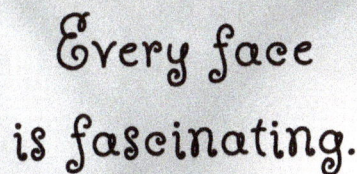

Every face is fascinating.

Sometimes you must wail
to get what you need.

A soft blanket
nestles you in heaven.

Mush is comfort food.

Wide-eyed wonder teaches all you need to know.

When you see something new, grab it.

Baldies are beautiful.

Bibs allow for total abandon.

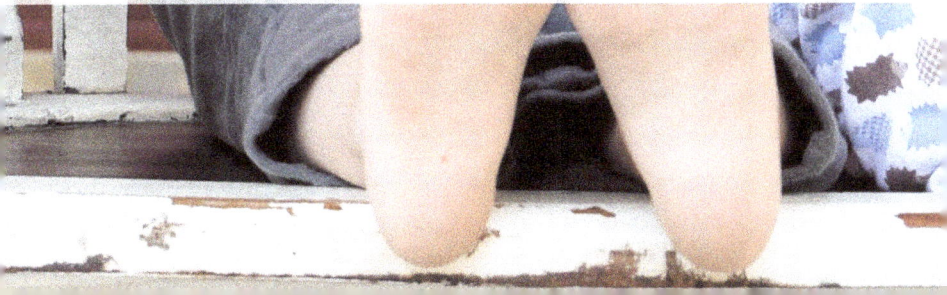

The life entrusted to you is a precious gift.

Playpens keep your toys within reach.

A smile is the sweetest part of life.

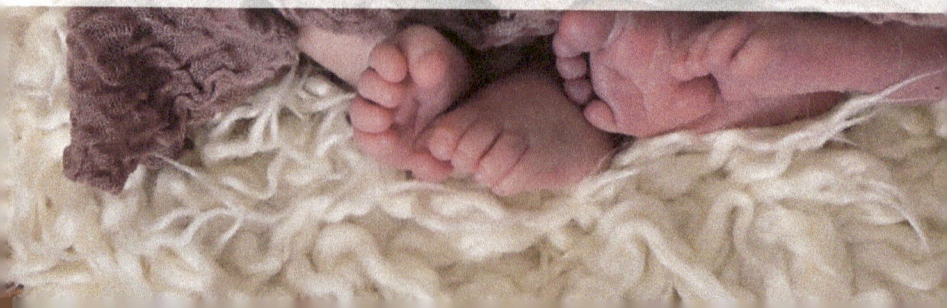

A trusting heart will adopt a loving person.

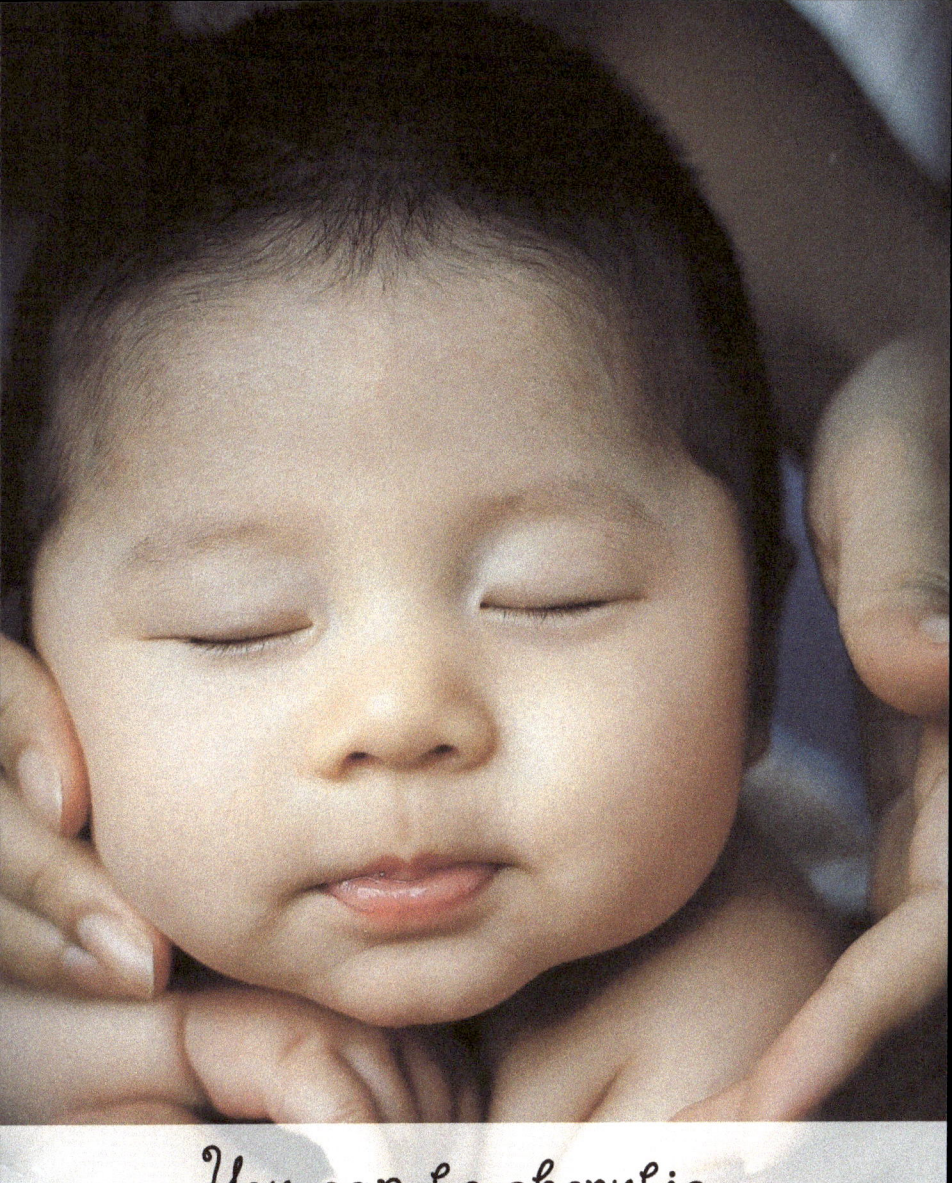

You can be cherubic without even trying.

A little spit up won't kill you.

When the going gets tough, squeal.

Toys will never replace playful interaction.

A fist just needs something to hold onto.

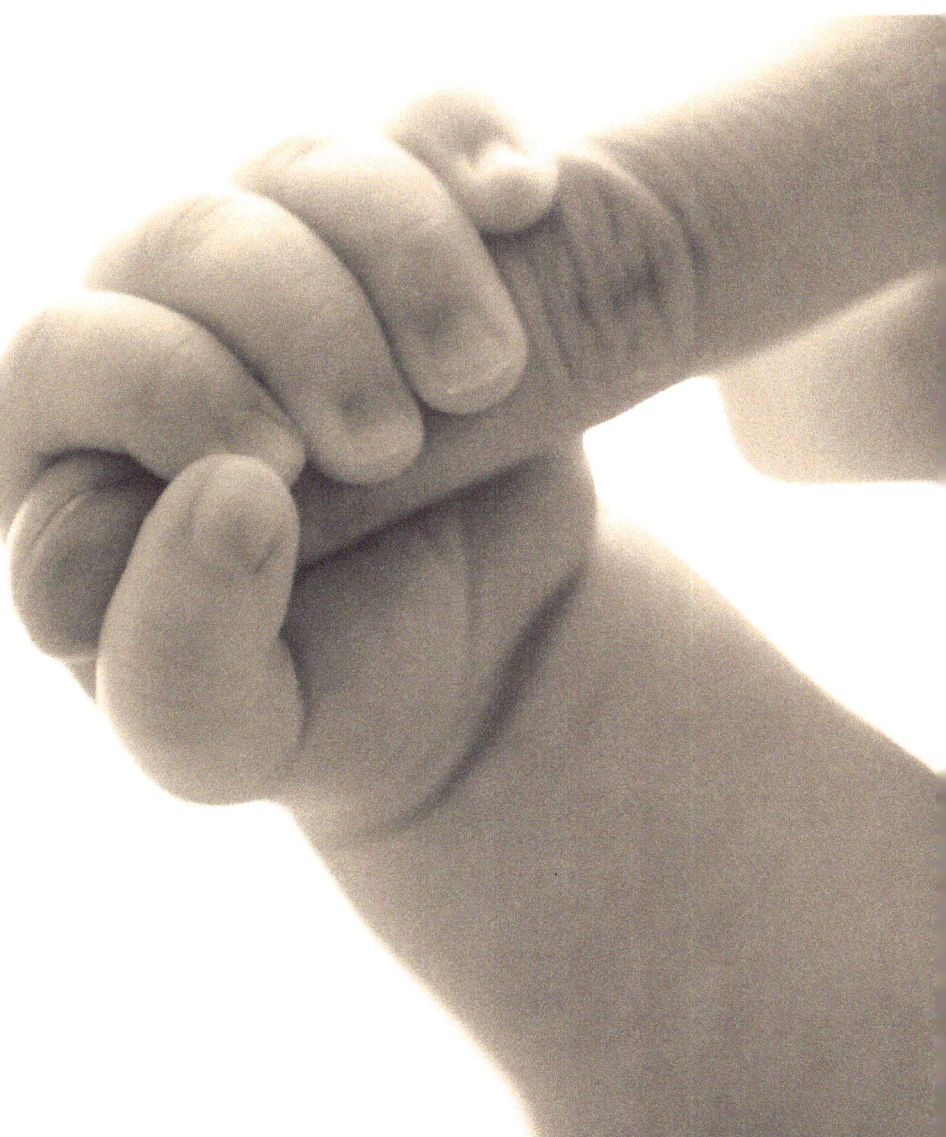

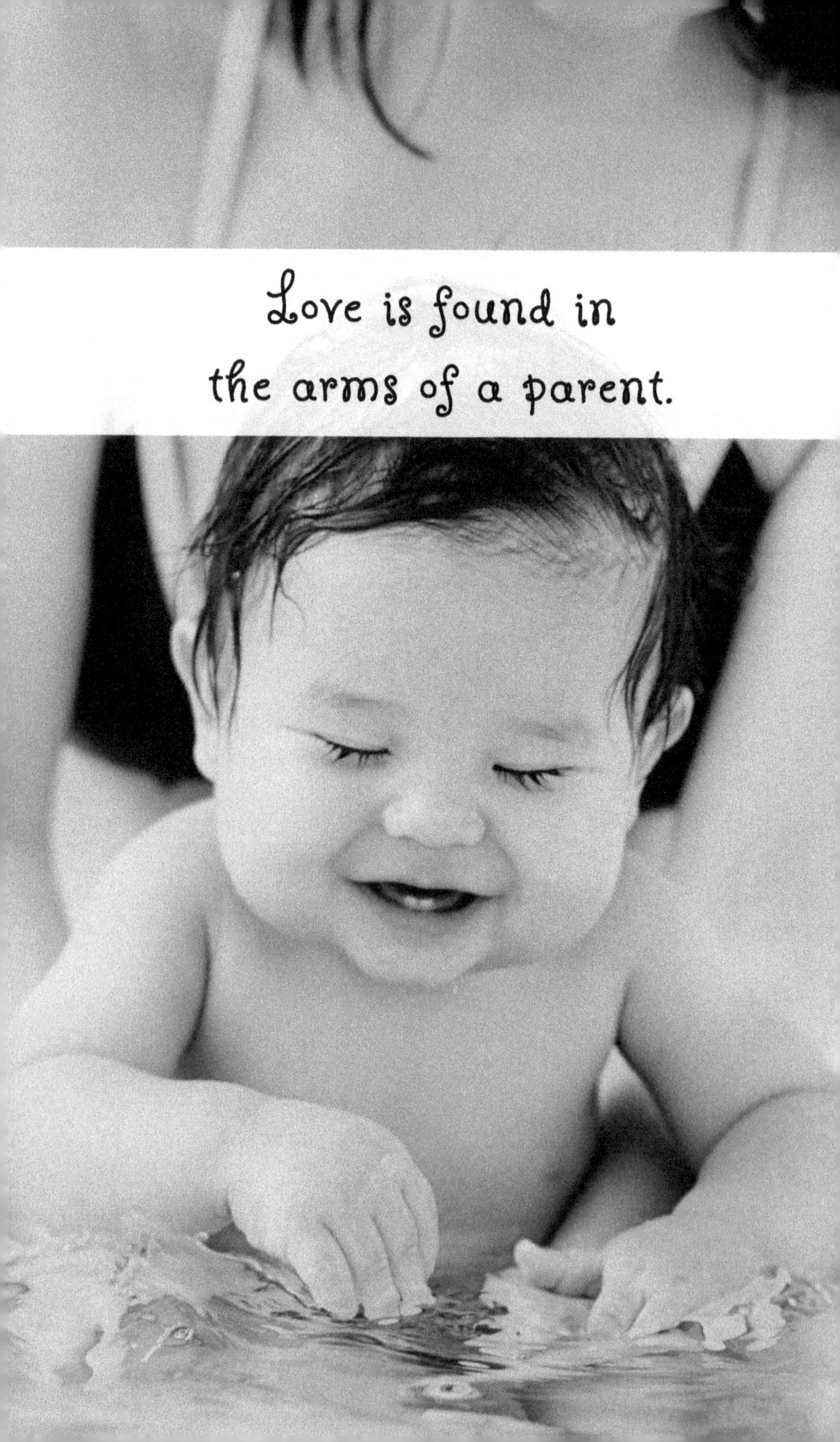

Love is found in
the arms of a parent.

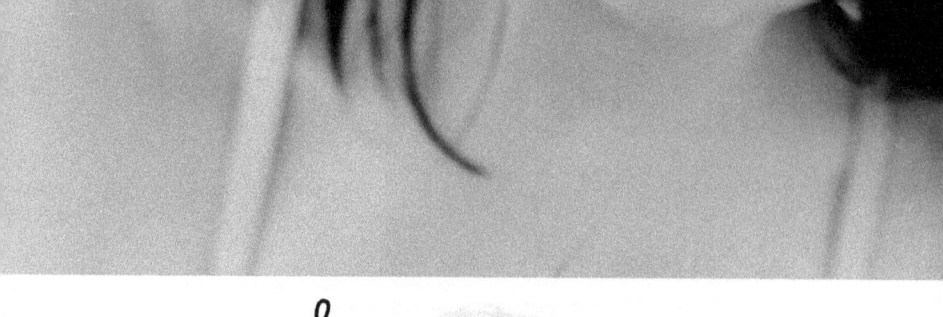

The bigger the mess,
the deeper the engagement.

Swaddling is a full-body hug.

A good burp releases whatever you don't need.

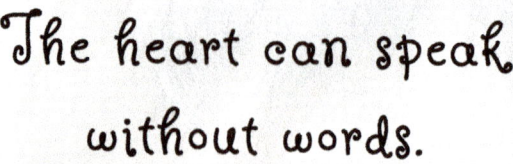

The heart can speak without words.

Your first steps
will always wobble.

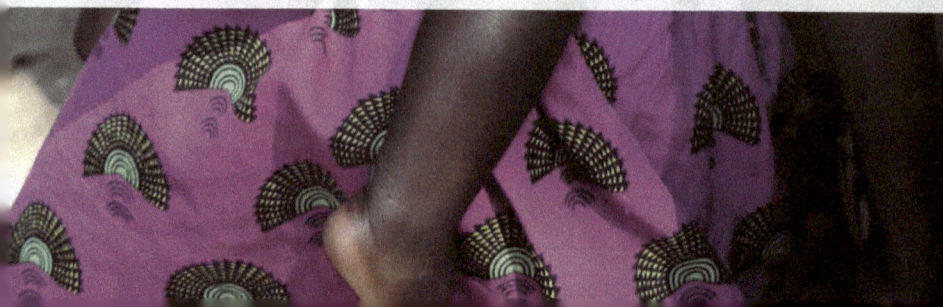

A sling keeps close that which you treasure.

A highchair provides a new perspective.

A teddy bear can be your best friend.

Warm milk is nature's sleeping potion.

Being fussy is a
sign of good taste.

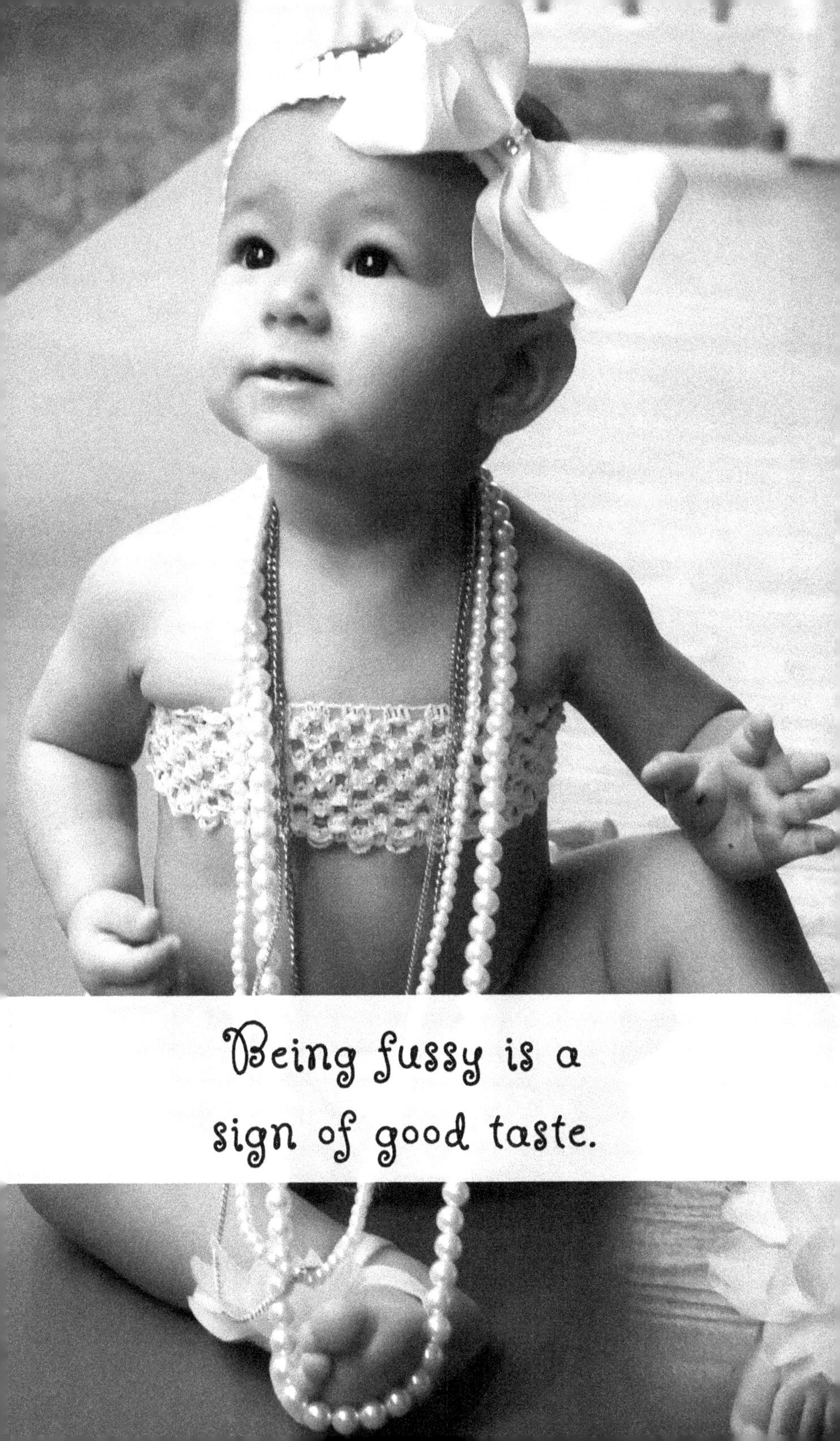

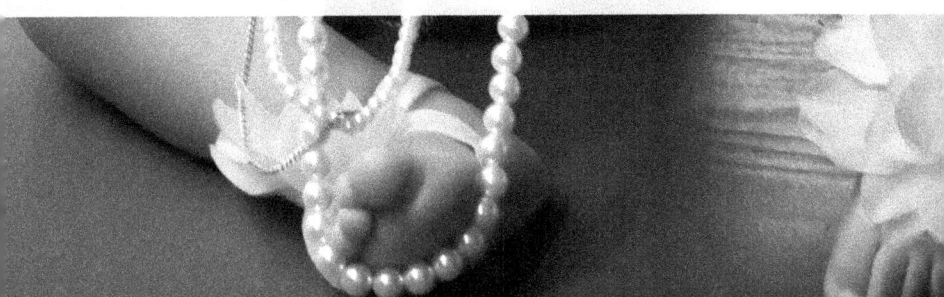

A tiny hand can form the strongest grip.

"Dada" and "mama"
are the stuff of songs.

Every sunrise lights a new adventure.

Vulnerability is an asset.

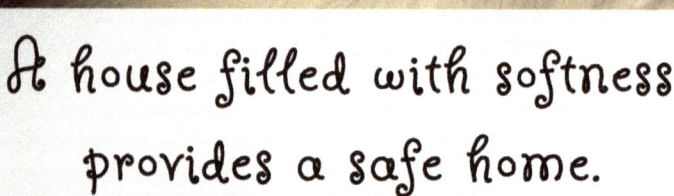

A house filled with softness provides a safe home.

Teething is a time of transition.

As you grow bigger,
so does the world.

You can exercise just fine
lying on your back

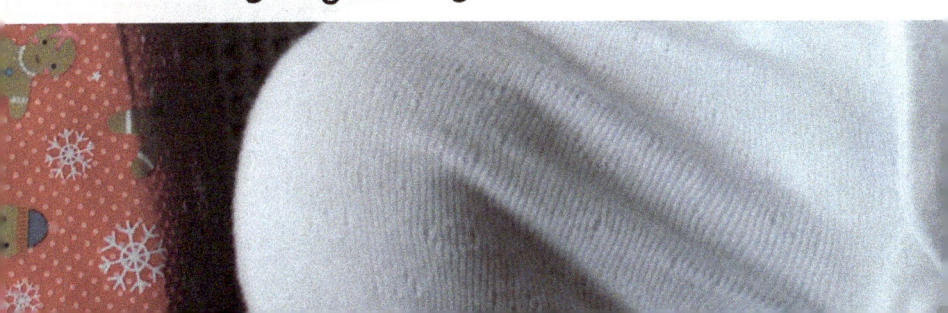

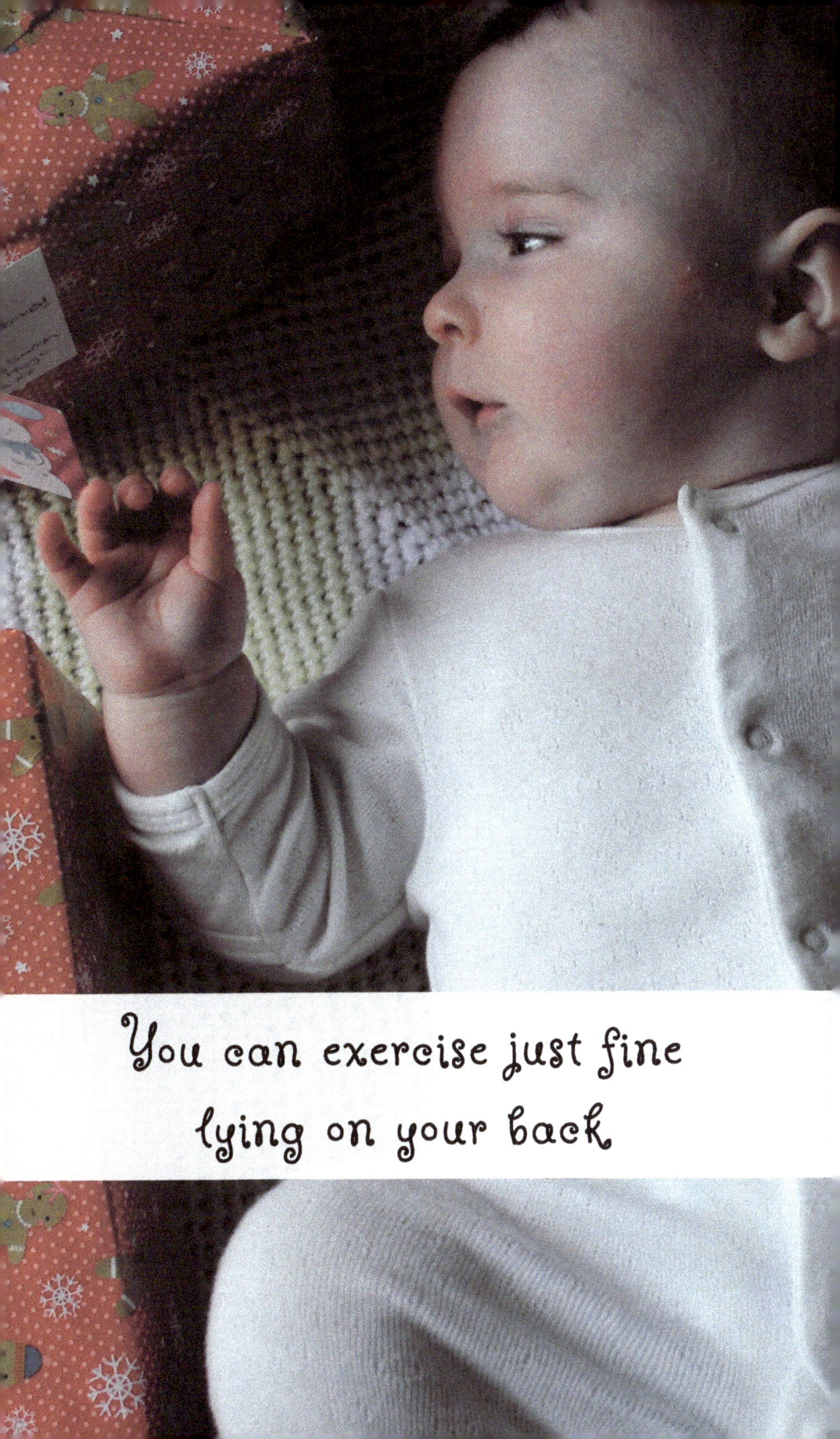

You will always receive everything you need.

Birthday cake should be eaten with both hands.

A family shining with love lights the path ahead.

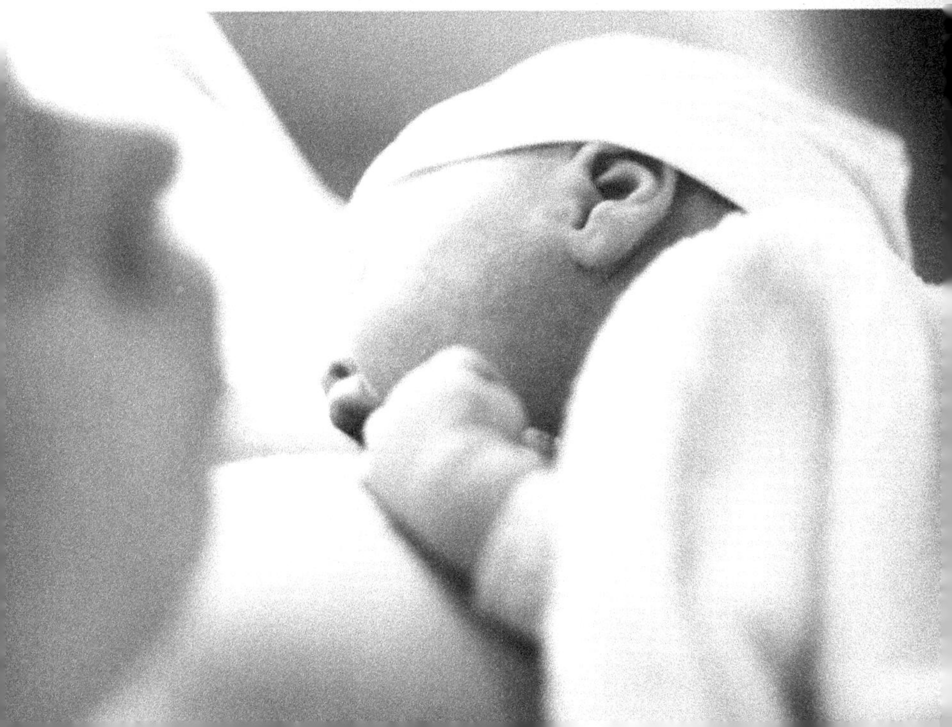

About the Author

Laine Cunningham's books take readers on adventures around the world. *The Family Made of Dust* is set in the Australian Outback, while *Reparation* is a novel of the American Great Plains. Her women's travel adventure memoir *Woman Alone: A Six-Month Journey Through the Australian Outback* appeals to fans of *Wild* and *Eat Pray Love*. Her work has received multiple awards including the Hackney and the James Jones Fellowship, and has been published by *Reed*, *Birmingham Arts Journal*, and the annual anthology by *Writer's Digest*. She is the senior editor of *Sunspot Literary Journal*.

Fiction

The Family Made of Dust
Beloved
Reparation

Nonfiction

Woman Alone

On the Wallaby Track: Australian Words and Phrases

Seven Sisters: Messages from Aboriginal Australia

Writing While Female or Black or Gay

The Wisdom of Puppies
The Wisdom of Babies
The Wisdom of Weddings

The Zen of Travel
The Zen of Gardening
Zen in the Stable
The Zen of Chocolate
The Zen of Dogs

Bikes of Berlin
Necropolises of New Orleans I & II
Ruins of Rome I & II
Ancients of Assisi I & II
Panoramas of Portugal
Nuances of New York
Glimpses of Germany
Impressions of Italy
Altitudes of the Alps
Knights Through the Ages
Utopia of the Unicorn
Portraits of Paris
Flourishes of France

www.ingramcontent.com/pod-product-compliance
Lightning Source LLC
Chambersburg PA
CBHW041959080526
44588CB00021B/2805